Ecosystems
Forests

by Nadia Higgins

Bullfrog Books

Ideas for Parents and Teachers

Bullfrog Books let children practice reading informational text at the earliest reading levels. Repetition, familiar words, and photo labels support early readers.

Before Reading

- Discuss the cover photo. What does it tell them?

- Look at the picture glossary together. Read and discuss the words.

Read the Book

- "Walk" through the book and look at the photos. Let the child ask questions. Point out the photo labels.

- Read the book to the child, or have him or her read independently.

After Reading

- Prompt the child to think more. Ask: Have you ever visited a forest? Have you seen videos or pictures? How would you describe it?

Bullfrog Books are published by Jump!
5357 Penn Avenue South
Minneapolis, MN 55419
www.jumplibrary.com

Library of Congress Cataloging-in-Publication Data

Names: Higgins, Nadia, author.
Title: Forests / by Nadia Higgins.
Description: Minneapolis, MN: Jump!, Inc., [2017]
Series: Ecosystems
"Bullfrog Books are published by Jump!"
Audience: Ages 5–8. | Audience: K to grade 3.
Includes index.
Identifiers: LCCN 2017000819 (print)
LCCN 2017002385 (ebook)
ISBN 9781620316788 (hardcover: alk. paper)
ISBN 9781620317310 (pbk.)
ISBN 9781624965555 (ebook)
Subjects: LCSH: Temperate forest ecology—Juvenile literature.
Temperate forests—Juvenile literature.
Classification: LCC QH541.5.T45 H54 2017 (print)
LCC QH541.5.T45 (ebook) | DDC 577.3—dc23
LC record available at https://lccn.loc.gov/2017000819

Editor: Jenny Fretland VanVoorst
Book Designer: Molly Ballanger
Photo Researcher: Molly Ballanger

Photo Credits: Alamy: FLPA, 13; blickwinkel/S Gerth, 14–15. Getty: George Grall, 16–17. Shutterstock: photka, cover; DutchScenery, 1; Eric Isselee, 3; Checubus, 4; dugdax, 5; Zadiraka Evgenii, 6; grynold, 8; Tracy Immordino, 9; Vahan Abrahamayan, 11; Pictureguy, 12; padung, 16; spiber.de, 20–21; Keattikorn, 23mr; Madlen, 23br; Beata Becla, 24. SuperStock: Design Pics, 6–7; Jason Langley/age fotostock, 10–11; Don Johnston/age fotostock, 18–19.

Printed in the United States of America at Corporate Graphics in North Mankato, Minnesota.

Table of Contents

So Many Trees!

A forest is full of trees.

It is shady here.

Look up!

The branches make a roof.

There are many kinds of forests.

Some are evergreen.

The trees keep their needles all year.

needles

Other forests have trees
that lose their leaves.

First the leaves
change color.

Then they fall.

See the bare winter branches?

9

In spring, new leaves grow.

Trees are homes for forest animals.

Birds make nests.

So do squirrels.

den

Look!

A bear makes a den
in the roots of a tree.

Its long claws
help it dig.

Trees are food.

A caterpillar
eats leaves.

A bird eats
the caterpillar.

Leaves fall to
the forest floor.

They break down.

That makes rich soil.

New forest trees
will grow.

Where Are the Forests?

**Much of the eastern United States is covered in forests.
New England is famous for its fall color.**

■ temperate forest

Picture Glossary

bare
Naked; not covered up.

needles
Tree leaves that are long, thin, and pointy.

caterpillar
An early developmental stage of a butterfly or moth.

roots
The underground part of a plant that absorbs water and minerals, stores food, and holds the plant in place.

evergreen
A kind of tree that has needles for leaves and stays green all year.

soil
Another word for dirt.

Index

To Learn More

Learning more is as easy as 1, 2, 3.

1) Go to www.factsurfer.com

2) Enter "forests" into the search box.

3) Click the "Surf" button to see a list of websites.

With factsurfer.com, finding more information is just a click away.